Catharse-is

About the Author

Steven Ogg is best known as an actor on a variety of popular television shows. From 2023's *Boiling Point* on the BBC, to his stand out roles on *The Walking Dead, Better Call Saul, Westworld, Snowpiercer, Broad City*, and *The Tick*. He might even be best known for his portrayal of Trevor Philips in the global phenomenon *Grand Theft Auto V*. Steven has completed filming numerous independent films and is currently in the throes of developing multiple projects from theatrical to film. Born in Calgary, Canada he currently resides in sunny South Pasadena, California.

Steven Ogg

Catharse-is

Vanguard Press

VANGUARD PAPERBACK

© Copyright 2024
Steven Ogg

The right of Steven Ogg to be identified as author of
this work has been asserted by him in accordance with the
Copyright, Designs and Patents Act 1988.

All Rights Reserved

No reproduction, copy or transmission of this publication
may be made without written permission.
No paragraph of this publication may be reproduced,
copied or transmitted save with the written permission of the publisher, or in
accordance with the provisions
of the Copyright Act 1956 (as amended).

Any person who commits any unauthorised act in relation to this publication
may be liable to criminal prosecution and civil claims for damages.

A CIP catalogue record for this title is available from the British Library.

ISBN 978-1-83794-277-0

This is a work of fiction. Names, characters, businesses, places, events and
incidents are either the products of the author's imagination or used in a
fictitious manner. Any resemblance to actual persons, living or dead, or actual
events is purely coincidental.

Vanguard Press is an imprint of
Pegasus Elliot Mackenzie Publishers Ltd.
www.pegasuspublishers.com

First Published in 2024

Vanguard Press
Sheraton House Castle Park
Cambridge England

Printed & Bound in Great Britain

Dedication

To my family and friends, I love you. To the multitude of artists from every medium that inspire me daily to share my truths and continue to tell stories, I love you and say thank you. I am very grateful for each of you reading this book, and for this opportunity to share my collection with you all.

Acknowledgements

Gord Downie for gifting us all and leaving me knowing that "Catharsis? My arse is capable of more flush…" And to every artist that has shared their work that make me want to continue to share mine.

Intro to Catharse-is

A collection of cathartic moments shared in my belief that the collective helps an individual to heal and to grow; embracing the journey to move through the difficult times with hope, at times a slight wink, and at other times with a smile, but never alone.

This book was born from a personal sketchbook; my Insta-book. An art installation project for me; largely intuitive, these cathartic moments rush in and thru me. We are born and we die alone, and in between hopefully experience and discover things that make us feel less alone.

This is my Insta-book.
This is Catharse-is;
my arse is capable of more flush.
Steven Ogg

Year One

Oct 31ˢᵗ 1:32 P.M.

One truth.
A sole's soul only.
One reality known to it alone.
Residing within the heart.
Weaving amongst the fissures.
Tall hedges in the maze
built by the hurtings
the conjectures/the guessers/the haters
joined together in their union of
D.K.W.T.F.T.A.T.A -
Don't Know What The Fuck
They Are Talking About-ers.
The unknown-ers disqualified.
The hurt can live aside the acceptance.
That lives on the property
within the maze
with the pond
with the soul swimming
next to the spotted koi
living in its water.

Nov 1st 9:06 A.M.

So much more of a rant and rave
I could set off upon.
A process that deserves exposure/transparency
its rightful place
at the bottom of the water
with the bottom feeders,
but I shan't.
Instead, I choose beauty.
Instead, I choose this.
Wading in creates the wave
worth the wait.
A splash suffice for some.
Submerged. All in.
Sheer beauty
welcomes a feeling of pansophy
of the emotions.
Taking qualitative intelligence
over quantitative aptitude
any day of the dip.

Nov 4th 5:16 A.M.

Crucified. Electrified.
Pecked at. Torn apart.
Love's lightness ironically illuminating
the evisceration.
The vultures' hyoid apparatus
working away.
Love's light reflected off the shiny,
bloody guts being torn out.
Pain as real as the crowd gathered
doing nothing.
Gawkers immune
to the vultures' lust,
but love's light
passing thru
a giant magnifying glass
held up in the back row
seers into the skin… sizzling.
Light. Dark.
Just a lovely photo folks…
So fucking relax!

Nov 7th 8:32 P.M.

Promulgated thru this.
Reverence for the process
which is that.
Sharing despite the shadows.
Experiencing in spite of feeling
a lack of silver at times.
That struggle
becoming the most powerful part
of the future story.
Told over and around.
Passed to learn from and to.
Tools to become more evolved.
Authenticity in complexity.
Takes more than just being a member
of the Wise Club.

Nov 9th 2:49 P.M.

Sitting in not sitting around
Not waiting for the moment
Not expecting an about face
Not seeing a change
Nor needing it from that
Sitting in this moment
Full life living it
Saddened by the nefarious greed
Enlivened by the love
Never those two shall meet
The darkness sits outside
The lightness sits inside me
Staying in opened to all.

May 9th 3:08 P.M.

The warmth found
in the septuagenarians
couples' hands embraced.
The glow found
in the person wearing a smile.
The early bedtime
to welcome an early day.
The morning brew
of Kicking Horse coffee.
The evening brew
of a mosaic IPA.
The morning yoga
activating and enriching.
The evening meditation
seeking and comforting.
The weekly therapy.
The daily reading.
Finding what works
not just to float the boat,
but to sustain the journey –
to rise above the turbulence
to give that hope
the bad/aches still exist

but enriching
the good-feeling
that goodness
to pass along and share.

May 8th 12:27 P.M.

Be kind –
to others/to yourself
Barriers between us –
be it a glass window
or insurmountable wall…
So… Tap Tap Tap

Some have beliefs/morals
remaining as solid
as the impenetrable barriers
seemingly never changing.
Nothing to do about either…
So…Tap Tap Tap

Sentiments like platitudes
when callous or ignorant
but truth resides in gratitude. –
Being positive in the moment
while optimism
resides in that unknown ahead…
So…Tap Tap Tap

April 24th 10:23 A.M.

Pumping hard
on the '70s stationary bike.
Blaring from the speakers –
Tainted Love then Painful Reminder.
Blasting down the back alley –
head jacket on.
Smells of smoke
from the bangers at the back door.
Peeing behind the garbage can
cause time was short.
Knuckles bruised
from this morning's fence.
Racing from and towards
an unattainable hill top
when remaining in one place.
So moving forward…
one pedal stroke
at a time.

April 17th 7:29 A.M.

A page a day
Torn out of the book
Left on the kitchen's table
Of an open house
To an open community
For every person
Passing thru the front door
On their journey
To the back
To take a moment
Within their multitudes of such
To peruse and possibly
To ponder;
its sense•its applicable nature
OR simply to be entertained.
And a page a day
May not keep sanity at bay,
but a sight more digestible
than an entire book at once.

April 16th 5:45 A.M.

Being happy
is not dependent on circumstances.
but they can sure help
Being in the moment
not co dependent
on those happening before or after.
but they sure can help
Pursuing passion
Living life to its fullest
Milking the teat
outta every experience
is a courageous choice;
not the simplest
not the easiest.
Being happy.
with circumstances/happenings
not always being
that sweet Vitamin D
from the sun's rays,
but rather
painful tattered shards
of sharp hail
raining down

from every direction.
To preach.
To proselytize.
To practice.
The first two
coming from many angles.
The latter
arriving when the eyes open.
Being happy now
takes nothing away
from the pain
or that which is a part
of your past or present.
Nor does a smile today
lessen the significance
of certain absence.
The work moving forward
is what it takes
to continue
to move forward.
Not stuck in the quagmire
surrounding you
from being happy.

April 9th 4:06 P.M.

Cracked window –
open heart.
A closed mind –
nothing changes.
An open book
can still be read.
Ending chapters
book still open
can still be read.
Books shut and never opened –
can't be read.
Keep the book open.
Keep the hands scrubbed.
Keep the mind/the heart open
see how we can still love.

April 7th 6:25 A.M.

Truths
What is
What are
Truths
Like love
It is known
Right in front
Present in hand
Truths
No energy wasted
No sickness spewed
No shit spread
Truths
Blue skies and a warm sun
A wave. A phone call. A smile.
Truths
like kindness
spread amongst the loving
give rise
to beautiful growth
despite
or is that
"in spite of"

the manure spread
within
the fertile soiled truths.
Truth. Kindness. Love.
Be kind.
Doesn't mean I am.
Doesn't mean
we all can't strive
nor shouldn't be
reaching, wanting, to being.
Anyone know a good fart joke?

Aug 30th 5:39 P.M.

On the bottom of my shoe –
where it belongs
carried around
for a couple days
its stench permeates.
Is it me?
No.
Just my shoe;
others shit.
Half dried now,
I move forward
having scraped the rest of it off.

It's not
what u r known for.
It's what you did;
that is what is remembered.
Don't be a piece of shit.
Be kind.
Smells better.

April 1st 9:09 P.M.

Isolated pre isolation
from what was
The norm shattered
from its onset
Never mind
the current state
Long before
we became separated
Thru a screen
from behind a window
Isolated from the isolation
Continue to do all we can
for each other
Even when not there
To be there
To repeat, "I love you"
To repeat, "You're my favourite"
To crack a smile
Even as the heart is heavy,
the spirits are not up,
and the tears are flowing,
and say, "See you tomorrow. Thank you for being my favourite. Love you."

March 29th 6:07 A.M.

Everything remained –
on the bridge of perhaps.
A dessan or croquis?
So many
with so little.
Too many
with too much.
Landscapes or abstracts?
Like the best advice given
of what it's like to have nothing
espoused from a wealthy mansion.
Taken for what is worth
and where it came from.
Splattered or thick gobs layered.
Interpreted as seen fit
by ones eyes only.
There's pain that uses you.
There's pain that you use.
On the bridge of perhaps
the easel is carried away.

Aug 16th 4:58 P.M.

Even if standing
in a steaming pile of shit
there are reasons to smile.
Even if hammered down
to feel like nothing
the morning's sun rises.
All you are
is everything you be.
Stay true. Stay you. Stay authentic.
Your path will find you
when you have lost it.
A good strong and delicious coffee
doesn't hurt either!

April 3rd 2:19 P.M.

48 years
576 months
17,520 days
420,480 hours
48 boxes being packed every day
576 bags to donate/recycle/trash
17,520 X 3 meals made here a day at least
420,480 emotions whisking around me
Countless memories
carried away.

Feb 16th 5:17 P.M.

Some things just suck.
Some things really don't suck.
Always seeing the beauty –
never a problem for me.
Feeling the lows –
can be a problem for me.
No stranger to the pain.
No foreigner to the love.
Such as it is.
Such as it goes.
Big boy pants. Sucking it up.
Dress it up six ways from Sunday.
We feel what we feel.
We live how we live.
And yes, I know all too well –
we all have a choice.
Use tools at hand.
To share. To express.
Not to glorify.
Only to reach out to say,
"I am here."
If I could… I would… We should.
I guess because sometimes –
I feel alone

I want others to know —
we are not.

Jan 25th 6:01 A.M.

That's the way – life is felt full on.
That's the way – natural beauty takes you.
That's the way – to feel love.
That's the way – heaven is here.
That's the way – any pain turns to pleasure.
That's the way – the shit goes away.
That's the way – to breathe.
That's the way – to know what's important.
That's the way – to reflect upon.
That's the way – the blues become blueER.
That's the way to be – grateful.

Jan 24th 7:33 A.M.

Magnanimous love.
Given unconditioned or all.
Gallant under the thatched roof.
Working with every tool available.
One set used differently.
Goldsworthy's stone wall impenetrable.
A platter of delectables/delicacies.
Baked/cooked laboriously with love.
Sharing all the ingredients –
an open recipe.
Left on the counter – for its party of one.
Megalopsychia pursued throughout.
Being what one is.
Never stopping it.
Magnanimous love.

Feb 17th 6:16 A.M.

The morning's first light.
Warmed by its renewal
of a new day.
Clouds scattered,
but the sun's will
shines right through them.
A clear pathway
illuminated.
So much easier
to see moving forward.

Year Two

Sept 20th 4:48 P.M.

My father –
I see you searching
I feel your love
I see your struggle
I felt your support
I see you lost
I hold your hand.
Without you saying,
"Go!
Work/school
will always be there."
I would never have gone
I would never have been
I would not be the man
I am today.
As you travel down
this insidious tunnel
where there is but one end
as for us all
I say THANK YOU!
I say I LOVE YOU!
I say, how lucky we are!

Sept 9th 8:08 A.M.

Always held out;
opened/outstretched
limb no longer asleep
embracing/embracer/embraced
when all has been attempted
when all is here
ready/willing/able
to meet yours.

Aug 22nd 5:12 P.M.

The same arms
that reach out to you
are the same arms
that wrapped around you.
Each of us left with less,
but each having gained
through the loss
through the pain
through the distance.
We each move forward.
We each look back.
Through the light
of the candle that keeps burning
I stand here
arms open
in your dark.

Aug 17th 6:39 A.M.

Closer to its end
than to life's beginning…
its lessons continually unfold.
The struggle for semantics
acceptance to letting go
has become
the complicated simplicity
of just living with the situation.
It is what it is
comes to mind often,
but swallowing that
can be as challenging
as digesting
that all will work out.
It may.
It may not.
So I circle back around
to living with what is.

Aug 2nd 6:12 A.M.

Existing in that space
and
being okay with that
is the bed
I want to sleep in.

What has been taken
away
will never be brought back.
What is important
now
is this momentum forward.
Never replacing
all that is lost.
Never making up
for all that I want.
Rather existing
in this happier place
where possible exists
where hope resides
where I find a smile
feel the love I have
rather

than the love I lost.
I have found
there is more good people
in this world
than the bad misplaced.
Seek good. Find good.
Focus bad. Stay bad.
Simple. Stupid.

June 25th 5:07 P.M.

A surreal scape
with piece of mind
missing from the heart
that void
the missed hug
no goodbye.
So everything
is perspective,
but sometimes
it's hard as fuck
to turn my head.
So it's
"until next time"
and it's
a Proust-ian farewell
a swan song
with these words
go poof!
these thoughts
go boom!
these memories
I cherish.

June 2nd 10:39 A.M.

These moments
when all is good
riding the restorative spirit
of the stunning natural world
all is believed
nothing is impossible
trusting in
the faith of it
with love flowing
with hope abound
proliferated
enhanced
highlighted
by its inspiration
the beauty exists
enough
so that even though
my arms remain open
and you are not there
I can still feel them
wrap around myself
and I am comforted.

June 20th 4:14 P.M.

To the forgottens
to the discounted
to the ignored
to the taken for granted
to the disenfranchised
to those doing their best
to those heading uphill
to the always DO-ers
to the being IS-ers
to them left behind
to not being recognised-ers
to those doing right
regardless of all the wrong
I see you
I feel you
there is a day for you too;
NOWDAY!

June 10th 5:24 P.M.

The exterior
belies the interior.
Not a "fake it till u make it"
bullshit.
You can enjoy
you can smile
you can be fully present
in every waking moment
but behind those curtains
and not a carpet
matching the drapes situation
rather an embrace
a full on commitment to it
doesn't reflect inside –
what's happening there.
Like all,
rather a choice
to put out certain things
to choose the song
to curate the gallery
in a manner that befits
the all
the joy

the sadness
the longing
the absence
the presence
the LIFE.

May 29th 10:11 A.M.

Now is not forever
but in this moment
I take
its beauty
its tranquillity
its inspiration.
The pain never leaves
but that moment
is not now.
Now is this moment –
now is okay.
Not my disposition,
but my appreciation of
and my gratefulness for
shall be my forever right now.

May 24th 4:54 P.M.

Carry on
another day
open hand
rests at the side.
A journey found
a journey lost
loving, gaining, losing
it can lift us up
it can keep us down.
Reaching out
to a hand not there
as my arm swings –
its momentum to carry on
to another day.
To carry on•To carry on•To carry on
Open handed
with its open heart
beating in its palm.

May 9th 6:47 A.M.

Everything so close
right there
any given moment
turning in the right direction;
for the view/for a vista
for the warmth of the sun.
A soothing passage
an inspiring breeze
a smooth branch of hope
carried in
with the forever tide.

April 30th 3:39 P.M.

Fallen from above
beauty dissipated.
Scattered thoughts
lying on shattered hopes.
Spread out•worn thin•veiled dreams
Thick black Doc Marten boots
pulverise the petals.
Liquified•mesmerized•hypnotized
Seeping over curb's edge
draining into the sewer it belongs.
From below a Pennywise
rolls his eyes/shakes his head;
"It all falls down and dies,"
he reiterates.
"It's how you choose to live."

April 24th 7:07 A.M.

After a loss…
(magnitude of such adjusted
to absence
to a broken heart
to youth
to innocence
to a…)
Becoming lesser than before
never quite able
to breathe back in all the air
that was taken
immediately following the loss.

Doing what one can
whenever opportunity is there.
To convince oneself
that it is all we can do;
to allow oneself
to live with failures
without sucking up
the last of the air
in a floor of half inflated balloons.

April 9th 7:26 A.M.

The fire
taken its toll
damage done
long past the date
of its burning down
the abode.

Few items remain
next to all lost;
things to collectibles
books to art
things•things•things
with meanings
with places
set in the past.

A complete rebuild
from the ashes
something will rise
some may say.

Remaining memories
faced with extinction

to protect
the undertaking.

The timbre of
bitching and moaning
with the same tenacity
as grateful and appreciative
of all that remains
of the burnt timber
left inside of me.

April 7th 2:43 P.M.

Blinded by the wrongs
unable to see the rights.
Darkened and burnt
the flicker lays buried
beneath the I-beams;
once sturdy and steeled.
Resistant to the fire's heat
now hot and reactive –
collapsed in on themselves.
No longer supportive
just a heap
burying me with their weight.
A once proud structure
reduced to this.

April 3rd 5:03 P.M.

Vitriords
spewed out
from a novocained
pie hole.
No one asked for the rain
on this Roman holiday
it just came down;
each word acidic
every thought vitriolic.
A delectatio morosa
fills the claw tub
holding its body
with the grounded
egg shells powdering
its surface
quickly destroying
its very existence.

March 18th 2:49 P.M.

The gait of the walk
reminds me
how little I know
outside of all these
f e e l i n g s.
My understanding
as low as my abilities
when nothing
seems to matter
any more
and the doubts
strut by
wondering
where all that went;
that productivity
that drive
that desire
to be • to do • to care
about finishing any of it.
So I watch
all of it
walk ahead
not really caring.

March 14th 5:28 A.M.

Sometimes
becomes a lot of the time
when I just want to hear you;
for you to call my name.
For me to take your hand;
to hold you.
The clock never turns back,
but to have a minute
of that time back when…
would be a moment
to fill my heart with joy.
Those moments gone now,
but never forgotten
and certainly become
more than just sometimes
that I crave something
of what was.

Feb 27th 9:19 P.M.

An immense rush
of gratitude
proceeds the show.
Melancholy's bony fingers
strum and pick
as sadness
maintains the rhythm.
Looking out
I see all the faces
of all those I love;
those now
those yesterday
those absent
those that keep my world
what it is.

Feb 20th 9:28 A.M.

That despite it all
I can still feel like this…
That despite the sun
I can be plunged into dark.
That despite the sheer beauty
I can just feel the ugly.
That despite the support
I can feel so unstable.
That despite such blessings
I can feel nothing but angst.
That despite all the words
I can just see a blank page.
That despite it all
I can feel nothing at all…
At the same moment
that I feel too much.

Feb 16th 6:11 A.M.

Impermanence of all
takes nothing away
from the moment now.
Rather engendering
each other
as suffering does
to happiness.

Things missing?
Of course,
but look at all I have.
A book. A fire. A roof.
A further list ongoing
to be grateful for.

Subduing and purifying
not sedating
the mind.
The focus abject
as strong as the concentration
guiding me towards its insight.

A moment moves on,
but replaced by another
replaced by another
replaced by yet another.

Be the dog. Be a flower.
It knows nothing else.
It owns being
just what it is.
And inspiration/beauty rises
from its existence.

Knowing who U R
alleviates the suffering
the pain of any judgement
from within or outside.

Jan 29th 6:45 A.M.

If you don't succeed
in being
you can't succeed
in doing.

Jotting down
the words
reflecting feelings/moods
expressing moments
getting it down and out.

In return –
safer passage
a sense of doing
a deeper understanding
healing benefits.

Could easily go under
(as I have)
the dark, crashing waves.
Sinking to the depths
trapped beneath
barely breathing

lashing out
drowning.

Could not as easily
dedicate to a practice
of well being
of rising back up
of reaching higher
to ride on top of those waves
to carry myself
to much higher ground.

Jan 26th 7:11 A.M.

A Hope For Change
(Broca's Area)

Terrible losses
transmuted.
Broken hearts/spirits
opened in compassion.
End points from despair
now supporting progress.
Loss into gain.
Pain into purpose.
Claiming hurt/anger
without being owned by them.
The greatest pain
teaching truths about ourselves.
Discovering
a hopeful attitude
an inner strength
an adventurous spirit
to bring enduring results.
(hope to share/share to hope)

Jan 17th 4:23 P.M.

Letting go/acceptance
far from forgetting
RATHER
closer to deepening;
its existence never wanes.
Read about it
till the words
are blue in my face;
intellectualize all I want.
Those two things actualized –
to let go
to accept
deepens all that.
The strength it takes
to do both of those
on something
so difficult
only proves how important it is
and THAT
will NEVER be forgotten.

Jan 3rd 1:45 P.M.

It's forward momentum.
It's movement forward.
Regardless of a hop/crawl/step.
What is worked towards
and what simply happens;
the chicken or the egg first?
Living responsibilities
as expressions
of the depths of our being;
it's authentic/inspiring,
but does it move the needle?
A hop/a crawl/a step…
keep moving forward.

"The soul grows by the measure of love it pours out."

Jan 6th 8:02 A.M.

The majesty of existence
with no one asking
to be here
to be who we are.
To BECOME who you are
is a choice you make –
we survive
we thrive
we hope
we suffer/we love
we laugh/we cry
we put on fancy socks
we take off dirty ginch
and we welcome
a brand new day.

Jan 16th 5:55 A.M.

I don't want to lose
that light
that appreciation
that moment of now
when I see the hope
when I feel the love
but stuck here
between depression
and frustration/anger…
I cannot hold nor reach
but simply point
to the demiurgic source –
that light.

Dec 31st 8:12 A.M.

The ambit of reflection
seen both ways.
Looking back to look within.
Looking forward to look ahead.

Open options
to sweet compulsions.
An existential urgency
to fulfill a lifelong dream.

"…love your crooked neighbour
With your crooked heart." W. H. Auden

"Good prose is like a window-pane." Orwell

Jan 2nd 6:16 A.M.

All behind some barrier.
All in front of some barrier –
worn slightly different
a mask/a fence/a gate
something to protect
some reason not to
enter/exit/proceed/prevented
with ways around/through
circumnavigate
tear it down/build from scratch;
always a way.
Find it!

Year Three

Sept 20th 4:12 P.M.

Taken off the page
not handed the book
nothing given
have to wait
waiting
having waited.
Proceeding on my own
I'd pass out
if I held my breath
on you;
knock my knoggin
or
frustrated,
a fist thru a wall
lacking all tools
the know how
but not the drive
to create
to grab those words
by the horns.

Aug 31st 9:09 A.M.

I work so hard
to do what I do
when I do it.
I work so hard
to live it all to the fullest.
I work so hard
to procure work.
I work so hard
to be kind/courteous/grateful.
I work so hard
to find that balance
between
dreams/hopes and grateful/appreciation.
I work so hard
I work so har
I work so ha
I work so h
I work so
I work s
I work
I wor
I wo
I w
I
WILL YOU?

Aug 18th 9:18 P.M.

I can't remember holding you,
but I know how much I love you
I can't remember details,
but I can feel your absence.

Then it hits me;
the pain
the frustration.

Tears turn to fists
sadness to rage
sobs to tantrums

Smashed plate
tossed bbq
torn tree

I destroy
to validate this pain
of missing you.

Aug 6th 6:42 A.M.

When did it become
so wrong
to want more
(not stuff!)
but those hopes/dreams?
Upon the fields of gratitude
when did it become
so wrong
to reach out
with open arms/outstretched hands?
When did it become
so wrong
to expect more from others?
Giving all of oneself
while continually
asking for
working towards
yet the same pleas/questions
seem to disappear
in that unanswered message.
When did it become
so wrong
to set boundaries

only to be met
with resistance
of the entitled attitude
from the others?
Why should these
feel so wrong
when all is right
and all you ask
is for mutual respect
is for a job to be done
with the same kindness
with the same hard work
with the same devotion
you give
to each/every day.

June 29th 6:06 A.M.

With the deadening
comes a reckoning
of maybe this is just how
it all plays out…
the roller coaster that was
now just a choo choo train
trudging along.
Moments of excitement
exhilarating downhill
or a sharp incline
but following these tracks
unable to deviate from their dullness.
Passionless steel
empty rail way ties
the cargo all emptied
because every conductor
said to let it go
but now there is nothing left
just fits and spurts
allowing these dull tracks
to guide me to the next town
where I am assuming
she will be on its platform
a bouquet of bananas
in hand.

May 22nd 7:01 A.M.

Blinding warmth
currents carried
on its silky surface.
Pains of yesterday
a passing lane
across the broken yellow line
now a distant place
as I move into this lane
to this place
of love felt
to love lived
fully and completely.

May 5th 5:57 P.M.

The darker days
the tougher ones
come and go much easier.
Existing within them
creates my path
of least resistance
thru them.
Inspiration helps me up
creative sources
unique voices
the visions, the words,
the artistry;
they all brace my chin
raising it higher
until I'm back
with head held high
and reinvigorated to move on.

April 30th 4:33 P.M.

In an entirely new place
surrounded by a fresh space
pants might be the same –
worn/battered/torn
shirt fresh as fuck –
crisp/original/NEW
Wearing it all with pride
acknowledging its whereabouts
feeling happy as fuck
to be here now
with you
with us
together in this wonderful space.

April 13th 5:18 A.M.

Am I enough
was I ever?
Will I ever be enough
for you
to turn around
to change direction
to just look back at me
once
to just listen to me
and hear my words
and see my tears
and feel my love
unwavering
unchanged
forever supporting you
forever loving you
forever here for you…
on Mars
on Pluto
on whatever planet
you or I be on
I am there –
open to you.

April 11th 6:12 A.M.

A twisted body
with a contorted face;
howling out his life!
A backdrop of such colour –
a depth of yellows
an incredible orange
a delicious purple.
A tireless witness
to lived experiences
observing this slow boil
of my consciousness.
REDUCTIO AD ABSURDUM;
the charm taking precedence
over life's atrocities.
The recourse to the density
of tragedy
of darkness
of man;
the plurality of moments.
Twisting in this chair
breaking myself in this bed
ruining myself in solitude
as my demons torment me
to the last drop

to the last drip
falling from my little head's hole.

March 6th 6:06 P.M.

Let it reign;
the toxic tears fall –
its muriatic acid wash away
everything now
creating something
better than
that we see
stronger than
that we be
its grey ash piled high enough
to see the sun rise beyond.

Feb 27th 8:18 A.M.

Harder as the anger mounts
more difficult
as the sadness grows
feeling more helpless
as shit worsens.
Glimmers exist
in actions
in voices
in dissidence
in the light
in that spark
igniting a fire within
burning away the darkness
incinerating the ignorance;
leading to tapasya's hand
guiding us to moksha.

Feb 21st 5:12 P.M.

The Augurs Lament –

Satiated by the work
lustful for opportunities.
Satiated by this moment
lustful for the next.
Satiated from the memories
lustful for new ones.
Satiated by your love
lustful for your flesh.
Satiated by the sunset
lustful for its rise.

Feb 18th 4:14 P.M.

Keep reaching out
continue holding it close.
Putting it out there
to pull it closer in.
To the wants
for the needs.
Holding on
to the rope
no longer a noose
now a tug o' war
between opportunities
and desires and dreams
VS
realities, gratefulnesses
and simply
what fucking IS.

Feb 8th 7:37 P.M.

Reflected in my past
lies
the sensibilities moving forward.
Steps measured by moments
informing my gait
based on where each foot
landed;
in a pile of shit –
to be avoided.
Shards of glass and thorns –
to walk around.
Lush fields of grass –
to cushion my soles.
Nature's waters
friends' and family's love/support –
the salve
rubbed on my calluses
to smooth and protect.

Feb 4th 3:16 P.M.

Seen only
in the reflection –
nothing of you here
in the now.
Taken away by the years
and
shackled to the past.
The emotions;
an omnifarious display
from sadness to anger.
They crest and swell
with a gurgle –
toiling with my sleep.
Sinking further
to lake's bottom
its glassy surface
irreparably shattered.

Jan 13th 5:04 A.M.

Waking up
in the dark
so as not to miss
its rise;
the hopes
the dreams
the colours
the anticipation
carried on
its beauty
its power.

Serving the memories.
Honouring the memories.
YET
not allowing those
to dictate my day.

I will leave that
to you –
slowly rising next to me;
your strength
becoming mine.